Choose Happy Journal

CHOOSE HAPPY JOURNAL

52 WEEKS OF *Guided Reflections* to **Cultivate Genuine Joy**

Sophia Godkin, PhD
THE HAPPINESS DOCTOR

To anyone who has ever wanted to be happier but didn't know how or was looking for it in all the wrong places.

Callisto Publishing LLC

Published by Callisto Publishing LLC C/O Sourcebooks LLC
P.O. Box 4410, Naperville, Illinois 60567-4410
(630) 961-3900

callistopublishing.com

Text by Sophia Godkin, PhD
Cover and internal design © 2026 by Callisto Publishing LLC
Illustrations © sini4ka/Shutterstock

Art Producers: Samantha Ulban and Stacey Stambaugh
Editor: Eun H. Jeong and Talia Platz
Production Editors: Nora Milman and Rachel Taenzler
Production Designer: Martin Worthington
Production Manager: Michael Kay

Printed and bound in the United States of America.
VP 10 9 8 7 6 5 4 3 2 1

This journal belongs to

"Happiness can come in a single moment. And in a single moment it can go again. But a single moment does not create it. Happiness is created through countless choices made and then made again throughout a lifetime. You are its host as well as its guest. You give it form, shape, individuality, texture, tone. And what it allows you to give can change your world."

—STEPHANIE DOWRICK, *CHOOSING HAPPINESS: LIFE & SOUL ESSENTIALS*

INTRODUCTION

Welcome to the *Choose Happy Journal*, your guide to discovering, understanding, and enhancing your capacity for happiness. Whether it's a desire to reflect on life, a commitment to self-care, a need for support in getting through a difficult time, or simply a longing to be happier that brings you here, you've come to the right place. Happiness is both a skill and a choice, which means you can learn to make the choice to be happy; this journal will inspire, encourage, and teach you how.

I am a health psychologist and genuine happiness and relationship coach for people all over the world. Nearly two decades ago, after having had enough with not being in control of how I felt day-to-day, I vowed to figure out this thing called "happiness" and dedicated myself fully to its wisdom and continual practice. I am so glad I did. Understanding and putting into practice the principles and habits of happiness has granted me relationships, work, and a life full of genuine contentment, both in good times and in bad. I am delighted and eager to guide you along your personal journey to genuine joy.

There are as many ways to approach happiness as there are reasons for doing so. My approach to happiness and what you'll be guided through in this book arose from both victories and mistakes made along my path to self-discovery and growth and from coaching hundreds of clients to do the same. I call it "happy from the inside out," and its goal is not just to help you understand and think about happiness but also to cultivate it naturally and incrementally from within.

My approach rests on three principles:

1. **Happiness is a skill you can learn.** Genuine happiness is a skill that requires understanding of and practice with both positive and negative thoughts and feelings, insights, inspired actions, habits, and goals. This journal offers plenty of opportunities for you to reflect, act, and cultivate this skill.

2. **Happiness is a state you have access to.** Genuine happiness is less about ecstatically jumping for joy and more about experiencing an inner sense of contentment. This contentment is already within you. Addressing challenges and obstacles to happiness makes it easier to access it. This journal provides many reflections and activities that will bring instantaneous joy, and many others that will help you cultivate greater joy over time.

3. **Happiness is possible for each and every one of us.** Everybody—no matter who you are, where you've come from, and what you've gone through to get here—has the ability to be genuinely happy. This journal guides you deeper into that understanding.

This journal provides guided prompts that build on one another for 52 weeks. Each topic serves as a focal point for the week, and each prompt is an invitation to reflect on your life, develop a quality, explore an approach, heal an old yet still-open wound, or have a happiness-raising experience. Go through the weeks of the journal in sequential order or in your own preferred order, do all of the prompts or pick and repeat some—do whatever works best for you.

My hope is that by using the *Choose Happy Journal,* you'll uncover a genuinely happier version of yourself with each passing day and week, and this experience will remind you that greater happiness is always possible.

Grab your mind, your heart, and a pencil or pen, and let's get started!

WEEK 1

BEING MY AUTHENTIC SELF

Bring to mind a decision you need to make. Write down the opinions that *others* have about what you should do. Silently say, "Thank you." Then take a moment to listen to your own inner voice. Write down what *you* think and feel is best for you.

To be who you truly are, you first need to know who you are without pressure to be anyone else. Ask yourself, "Who am I when I am not trying to be somebody I'm not?" and "Who am I when I am just being me?" Jot down your thoughts.

As you move through your day, make a conscious choice to show up as exactly who you are, nothing more and nothing less. Write about what it means for you to show up and be real. At the end of the day, reflect on how it went.

Your true self is who you are meant to be, and you don't need to apologize for it. If it feels right to you, write a short apology to yourself for one or two of the times when you apologized for being who you are.

What thoughts and habits have you adopted to support the vision of who you think you're *supposed to be*? What is one thought or habit you would be willing to let go of so that your life more closely aligns with your own vision of who you *are and want to be*?

Who do you know in real life (or a celebrity or fictional character) who is unafraid to be themselves? What do you admire about them? How can their way of being inspire you to more consistently be yourself?

What is one quality you have tucked away or compromised on because you thought others wouldn't accept you because of it? Would you be willing to put on your courage cape and display that quality in some way today? If so, how?

WEEK 2

FEELING GRATEFUL

What's one good thing that happened today? What made it feel so good? Write about it, and share it with a colleague, partner, or friend.

Make a list of things you love. Write down, "I love ________," and keep filling in the blank until you've reached 10 or you feel complete, whichever comes first. Look over the list and feel a deep sense of appreciation for all you have in your life.

It is said that a grateful heart is a magnet for miracles. Dig deep into your heart. What is something positive that came out of an otherwise negative experience you had recently? See if you can hold both the challenge and the opportunity of this experience.

Write down five things that you've been grateful for over the past three days and why. As you're writing, really take the time to feel appreciation in your mind, body, and soul. How does noticing things to be grateful for affect how you think and how you feel?

Make today a day of appreciation—for yourself! As you go about your day, take time to appreciate qualities of yours that you've taken for granted. What qualities of yours are worth appreciating?

Take a walk outside and practice gratitude for what you notice—the blue sky, the warm sun, the beauty of your surroundings. What is it like to feel grateful for things that you may otherwise have missed?

Write a thank-you note to someone who made a meaningful impact on your life in some way but who you haven't thanked properly. Read the note to them in person or via phone or video. How did it affect you to share this deep gratitude with them?

WEEK 3

CULTIVATING HOPE AND OPTIMISM

What does it mean to you to have hope and optimism?

What is one unpleasant thing you've been telling yourself repeatedly about the future? Knowing that it isn't true (because no one can really know the future), write the story you want to believe right now. For added hope and optimism, read this to yourself every morning for the rest of the week.

What are three specific things that have gone well recently? What does this suggest to you about the possibilities that exist for your future?

Imagine your dream life coming to fruition 10 years from now. How does it feel? How does it look? What does your family life look like? Your romantic life? Your friendships? Your career? Your health?

What are a few times in your life when important "doors," or opportunities, closed and other "doors" opened?

The next time something unpleasant happens and you notice yourself catastrophizing ("My whole day is ruined!"), challenge yourself to put things into perspective and reframe the situation. What turned out well because this one thing didn't go your way?

You can't be both worried and optimistic at the same time. Which attitude will you choose for today, and why?

WEEK 4

STRENGTHENING MY RELATIONSHIPS

Ask yourself, "How do I tend to show others that I appreciate them?" and "How can I do more of this for the people who mean the most to me?" Write down your reflections.

Pick one person you are close to. How can you make this person a priority and designate specific time in your schedule for them this week?

Today, as you go about your day, find one encouraging thing you can say to people you are close to. Later, reflect on and write about how showing encouragement affects your relationships.

Choose a friend or family member whose role in your life is meaningful. Share something with them that you've been feeling vulnerable about. How did it feel to reveal something about yourself to this person? How did it influence the bond between you and them?

Choose one person who matters a lot to you. Have a conversation with them this week that gives them a chance to talk about whatever is on their mind without feeling judged. How does showing openness and understanding impact your relationship?

Think of a relationship that could use some improvement. Reflect on what it would mean to bring it from a perspective of "me" (what I need and get from the relationship) to one of "we" (what we both need and get from it). Is there a step you can take this week to help the relationship get there?

Choose one person in your life you would like to have a stronger relationship with. What is one way that you can be a better friend to this person? How can you share yourself and your time with them? (See page 166 for additional resources on establishing stronger relationships.)

WEEK 5

CAPITALIZING ON MY STRENGTHS

What are a few of your strengths (things that come naturally to you)? Write about your strengths and how you use them in your life. (If you're not sure what your strengths are, ask a loved one.)

Choose one of your strengths. Write about how you can use this strength in a new way today, whether at work, at home, with your partner, or with friends.

Does your job allow you to use your strengths? Brainstorm a few ways that you can use your strengths more at work.

Think of a problem you currently have. How can you use your strengths to help yourself manage or overcome this problem? Jot down a few options and put one of them into action today. Later, reflect on how it went.

Pick one of your strengths and set an intention to use it when interacting with other people this week. How will you use it? How do you think doing so might affect your work and home lives?

Everyone has a gift to give. Considering what you know about your strengths, what is a gift that you have to offer the world? What is one way you can offer that gift in a small or big way today?

Take 10 to 15 minutes to plan a specific, achievable goal for yourself that is built upon one or more of your strengths. How does knowing that this goal was built on your strengths affect you?

WEEK 6

ACCEPTING ALL OF ME

What parts of you can't be loved by yourself yet? Why?

It's okay if you don't love all of yourself yet. What are five things that you sort of like about yourself?

What would it mean to embrace yourself as you are—to allow yourself to be who you are right now, without judgment or pressure to change or fix anything?

Is there an aspect of your appearance that you have trouble accepting? Rather than hating it or urging yourself to love it, what if you took a neutral approach? Write about this part of your appearance from a neutral perspective (e.g., "I appreciate everything my body does for me and accept it regardless of how it looks.").

____

____

____

____

____

What is one part of yourself that you wish would go away (e.g., the parts that procrastinate, worry, or criticize others)? Put your hand on your heart and say, "All parts of me are okay, even this one." How does it feel to stop wishing this part of you away?

____

____

____

____

____

Think of a quality you rejected or wished to get rid of in the past. Write it a message of kindness. Let it know that though you can't fully accept it right now, you're not giving up on being more at peace with it. What is it like to allow rather than fight this part of you?

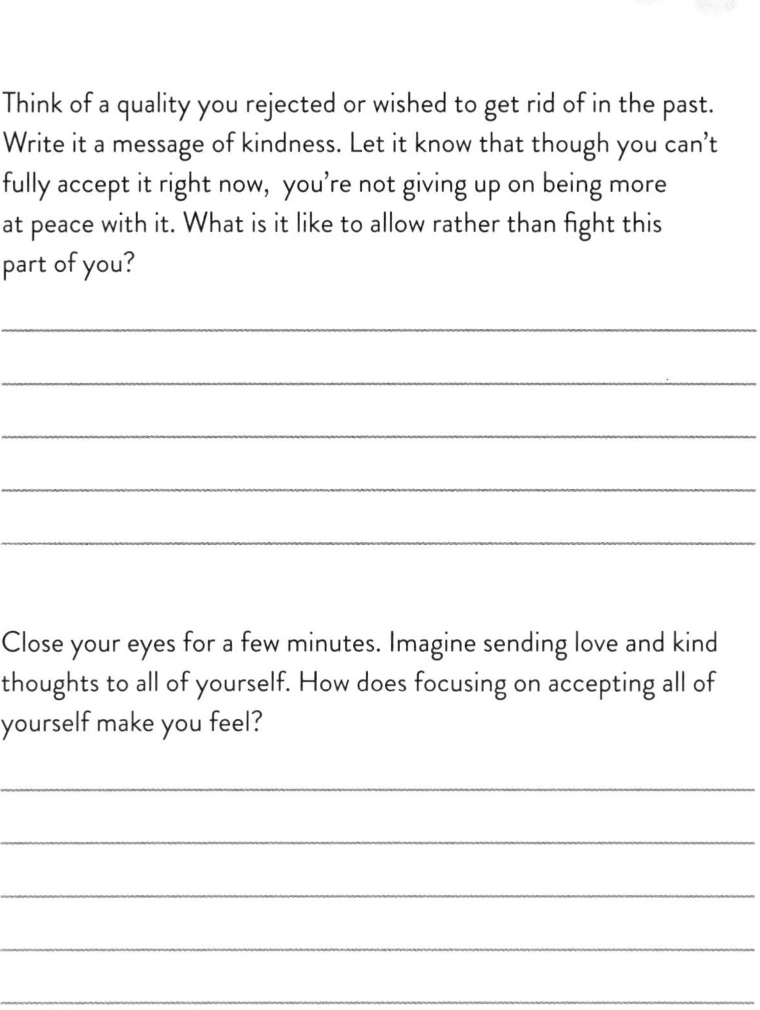

Close your eyes for a few minutes. Imagine sending love and kind thoughts to all of yourself. How does focusing on accepting all of yourself make you feel?

WEEK 7

PRACTICING SELF-CARE

Take some "me" time. Dim the lights, place your hand on your heart, and watch your chest rise and fall with each breath. Afterward, record any thoughts or feelings that came up for you.

Turn inward. What are three things you need right now to help you function at your best emotionally, physically, and/or spiritually? How can you take care of one of these needs right away?

Turn on your favorite song. Dance to it, sing along with it, or simply listen to it. Then write down what the rhythm or lyrics mean to you and how the song made you feel.

Saying no can be a way to honor your own feelings and needs before honoring those of other people. What is one thing you can say no to this week, and why?

Set a timer for five minutes. Find a comfortable place to sit, and invite yourself to let go of any tension you may be holding in your body. When the timer goes off, reflect on whether resting can be a productive thing to do, even for a short time.

Give yourself permission to pause. Notice and bring some understanding to how you're feeling by labeling your emotions (e.g., nervous, joyful, or content). What is a simple way that you can attend to one of these emotions (e.g., take a breath, journal about it, or talk about it)?

Jot down some of your priorities for the week. Are you on that list? If not, put yourself on there. Write down a few things that prioritizing yourself can help you achieve and embrace in your life.

WEEK 8

CULTIVATING SELF-COMPASSION

Think of a time you messed up. Write down, "Messing up at ______ doesn't make me a bad person." Then write some kind words you can offer to yourself about the experience, and say them out loud. How does it feel to offer yourself compassion for your mistakes?

What are you involved in right now, personally or professionally, that may be challenging? How can you be a little nicer to yourself during this challenging time?

Reflect on your day. What went as expected? What didn't go as expected? How can you show compassion to yourself for the things that didn't go as planned? (See page 166 for additional resources on self-compassion.)

Bring to mind an ambitious goal that you want to achieve. What would it mean for you to stop rushing, slow down, and go toward your goal only as fast as the slowest part of you feels safe to go? What would you need to do differently? How can you honor that part of you today?

What is a past failure you've had trouble accepting? Remind yourself that everyone fails at something at some point and that, like you, many feel inadequate, sad, or disheartened when they do. How does it feel to know that you're not alone in this experience?

What is something you've judged yourself harshly for, even if you had little control over it? How can you offer yourself understanding for this experience—and the shame that may have followed it—in the same way you would offer it to a friend?

Today, try on the idea that you deserve to treat yourself kindly, no matter what. What would it be like to treat yourself kindly, even when it comes to an undesirable quality you have or something you did that you regret?

WEEK 9

BEING PRESENT TO MY EVERYDAY LIFE

For a few minutes, pause and focus on your senses. Ask yourself, "What can I see, smell, and hear? Who and what is around me? How do I feel?" Reflect on the experience.

The next time you catch yourself imagining a miserable future, invite yourself back to the lovely moment right in front of you. How does it feel to move from worrying about the future to living in the present?

Today may be a good day or not such a good day. What one thing can you find to focus on or enjoy today instead of spending the day just hoping for a better tomorrow?

Prepare a meal. Turn off the TV, and put your phone away. As you eat, be present to the smells, textures, and tastes of the food. What is it like to connect to your senses while doing something that you do every day?

Slow down today. Pick a half hour to focus on doing one single task at a time. Do each task with awareness rather than on autopilot. When you're done, reflect on the difference between being present and not being present to your day-to-day life.

The next time you are having a conversation, really listen to the other person rather than thinking about what to say next. Does it feel different to engage in conversation with presence instead of anticipation? Reflect on and write about the experience.

Set a timer for two minutes. Close your eyes and visualize where you've been this past year. Set the timer for another two minutes and visualize where you're going. Then set the timer for five minutes and enjoy where you are. Reflect on and write about the experience.

WEEK 10

NAVIGATING MY THOUGHTS

What is one assumption you're making about what is possible for your life that is negatively impacting you (e.g., "I can't possibly find a partner who will love me for me.")? What would happen if you abandoned this assumption and adopted a different one for a while?

Our thoughts are rooted in our beliefs. What is one belief you have about yourself that makes you not feel good (e.g., "I am not smart enough.")? Consider whether that belief is totally true. Are there times when it hasn't been true?

Ask yourself, "What is another unsupportive belief I have about myself? Where did it come from? Who would I be, what would I do, and how would I feel without it?" Record your thoughts.

Identify a thought that's making you feel down. Ask yourself, "Is it a fact? Are there other possibilities that might be true?" Write down another possibility that may also be true. How does making space for alternative possibilities affect how you're thinking and feeling?

Take five minutes to think about a part of your life that is going well right now. How does it feel to focus on the good things more, not less? Spend some time reflecting on and writing about this.

Think of and write down an overgeneralization you made recently about a negative situation (e.g., "I will never succeed!"). Now turn it into a statement that makes fewer assumptions (e.g., "It was just this one time."), and remind yourself that just because something happened once, it doesn't mean that it will happen again. Reflect on and write about the experience.

Have you ever noticed yourself thinking that nothing ever works out? Invite yourself to not rush to conclusions but instead find a thought that is less definitive (e.g., "That was tough."). How does it affect you to view a negative experience in gray rather than black-and-white terms?

WEEK 11

SHOWING MYSELF KINDNESS

What is one small step you can take to shift from self-criticism to self-kindness and lovingly put yourself first this week?

When was the last time you gave yourself credit for something? At the end of today, look back on the day and acknowledge what you accomplished, no matter how small. Write about your accomplishments—boast about yourself!

Fill in the blank: "If I were listening to and meeting my own needs right now, I would ________." Provide as much detail as you can.

Think about a time when someone you love felt dissatisfied with their life. What did you do and say? What tone did you use? Write to yourself about your progress in life using that same tone. What is it like to treat yourself in the same way as you would treat someone you love?

Make a list of the "have-tos" and "shoulds" that you place on yourself (e.g., "I should be further ahead in life."). Notice how they make you feel. Now develop a kinder alternative to each "have-to" and "should" that you can take with you through the rest of the week.

Today, check in regularly with yourself at least four times. (Set a reminder on your phone if you need to.) Pause and ask yourself, "How am I feeling?" and "What do I need right now?" At the end of the day, reflect on and write about what you learned.

Write a short letter to yourself. Let yourself know that you see your joy and struggles and that you hear your worries and concerns. Include anything you need to hear today, and take a few moments to actually feel it. How does it feel to be seen, heard, and cared for by yourself in this way?

WEEK 12

FEELING MY FEELINGS

Ask yourself, "How am I feeling?" Give yourself permission to be honest and write until you get everything out. (Continue on a separate sheet of paper, if you'd like.) How does it feel to give your feelings a space to exist?

The next time you feel a difficult emotion, ask yourself, "How am I feeling?" and name the emotion. Then tune in to how this emotion feels in your body. What are the physical sensations that accompany this emotion (e.g., pressure in the head or tightness in the chest)?

The next time you're feeling sad, frustrated, or angry, instead of telling yourself you need to be happy in that moment, let yourself feel how you feel. How does it affect you to know that you don't need to be positive all the time?

Another time you're feeling a difficult emotion, ask yourself, "Why might I be feeling this way?" Then write down a few statements to normalize the emotion (e.g., "It makes sense that I would feel this way because . . .").

Set a timer for 10 minutes and allow yourself to feel (rather than judge or deny) your feelings, no matter what they are. With each feeling that arises, tell yourself, "There is nothing wrong with how I am feeling. All my feelings are valid." Reflect on how it felt to feel and validate your feelings.

Feeling your feelings is a brave act. What is a feeling that you've been avoiding or suppressing? What feels scary about the potential of feeling it? How can you hold this feeling of being afraid with self-compassion?

What is the difference between feeling your feelings and acting on them? Between talking about your feelings and acting on them? Are there times when it's appropriate to feel your feelings without acting on or expressing them?

WEEK 13

CONNECTING TO MY BODY

As you awaken, stretch your arms high and take a deep breath. Then stretch your arms open wide as you continue to breathe. Repeat this several times to get your blood flowing. Then ask yourself, "How does connecting to my body shape the rest of my day?" Jot down your thoughts.

Close your eyes and ground yourself in your body for 10 minutes. Feel your feet as strong roots that support you in everything you do. Visualize these roots supporting you throughout this week. When you open your eyes, jot down what it means for you to feel supported this week.

Celebrate what your body can do! Take 30 minutes today to move your body intentionally through exercise, yoga, or some other movement. What are 5 to 10 things that your body makes possible for you in your life?

For 15 to 20 minutes today, do some form of movement that feels good and brings you joy. How did this conscious movement affect your mind and your body?

For 30 minutes today, move because you want to. Go for a walk or a bike ride, play an active game with yourself or a loved one—whatever works for you. Write down your thoughts immediately afterward.

The next time you feel stressed or worried and notice your heart racing, close your eyes and gradually relax each part of your body. Did relaxing your body affect the momentum of your mind? What did you notice?

How is your body feeling? Are there any areas of tension or pain? Devote 10 minutes to acknowledging and easing any tensions through movement, breathing, and/or meditation. How can you pay attention to the way stress shows up in your body throughout the day?

WEEK 14

COMPARING MYSELF TO OTHERS

Unrealistic reference points (e.g., Photoshopped fashion models) can make us feel bad, while reasonable ones (e.g., ads showcasing people of all shapes and sizes) can make us feel better. How can you be mindful about the kinds of reference points that are coming into your awareness through the things you watch, read, and listen to today?

It is said that comparison is the thief of joy. Who are you comparing yourself to, whether in real life or on the Internet, and how does that make you feel? Write about one small step that you can take to accept yourself more today.

Today, every time you begin to compare yourself to someone else, pause, remind yourself that you cannot compare apples and oranges, and invite yourself to embrace the idea that you are good enough as you are. How did this make you feel?

Take 10 minutes to go through your social media accounts. Change the degree to which you can see the accounts, if at all, that lead you to feel "less than" or that cause you to compare. After a few days, journal about any differences that you notice in your mood.

The more grateful you are, the less likely you are to make self-defeating social comparisons. Write down 5 to 10 things about yourself and your life that you are grateful for.

Decide on and write down five to seven elements that make up the "ruler" you will use to measure your own progress regardless of what anyone else is doing. Take this "ruler" with you and use it throughout your day.

For a few minutes, close your eyes and contemplate the idea that life is not a race, and forward is forward regardless of your pace. When you open your eyes, reflect on how this idea might translate into your own life.

WEEK 15

UNDERSTANDING MY INNER CRITIC

Get curious about your inner critic. If you could step into its shoes, what do you think you would find out about why it judges and criticizes you sometimes?

What is one thing your inner critic has judged you for lately? Imagine a safe, comfortable space where you can be with both your inner critic and your inner champion (we all have one). Write out a brief dialogue between them, letting each one voice its opinions. What is it like to give equal attention to your inner critic and inner champion in this way?

If both your inner critic and inner champion had equal reign over your life, what words could you add to your inner dialogue to empower yourself more (e.g., "I can" or "I'm good enough")? What words could you be mindful of reducing from your inner dialogue (e.g., "I can't" or "I don't do anything right")?

The next time you hear your inner critic, recognize that it is trying to protect you. Rather than arguing with it, try to connect with it. Ask yourself, "How is it trying to protect me?" and "What might it be trying to protect me from?" Write down your thoughts.

Think back to a time when you judged yourself harshly. Then write a note to your inner critic acknowledging that it was simply trying to keep you safe. Thank it for its good intentions, and let it know that it's been an important aspect of who you are.

Today, recognize the voice of your inner critic. Does it sound like your mother? Your father? Someone else? What is it like to recognize this voice as not your own and realize it comes from someone who has their own inner critic?

Sometimes people may judge or criticize you. Using what you learned through this week's journal prompts, how can you not be one of them?

WEEK 16

SPENDING TIME, MONEY, AND ENERGY

Invest some money today in an experience like a nice meal, a concert, or a movie—not a material possession. How did spending money on this experience affect you?

How much energy do you typically allocate to your family, friends, goals, personal and spiritual growth, health, and leisure activities? Is the amount of energy you allocate consistent with how important each one is to you? If not, what is one thing you can do to more consciously align your time with what is most important to you?

Designate some money as money you will spend on someone else. Then go and do it. How did it feel to spend money on someone else?

Dedicate 30 to 90 minutes this week to spending time with friends and family (in person or by phone). What was it like to set aside special time to share your life with others? Is this something you want to do more of on a regular basis?

The next time you have the choice between (a) working more hours and making more money or (b) working fewer hours and making less money, consider choosing option b (assuming your basic needs are met). What can more time give you that more money can't?

What, if anything, has been draining your physical and/or emotional energy lately? What can you do to replenish your energy today? And how can you conserve your physical and emotional energy to prevent feeling drained in the future?

For a few minutes, close your eyes and visualize activities that are personally meaningful to you. How can you optimize your days with activities such as these and minimize the amount of time you devote to less meaningful ones, if even just a bit?

WEEK 17

ACKNOWLEDGING MY WORTH AND POSITIVE QUALITIES

Ask yourself, "What's the best decision I have ever made, and why?" As you write about it, let yourself revel in your ability to make good decisions.

Ask yourself, "What am I excelling at right now that in the past I couldn't do?" Write down your thoughts.

Ask yourself, "What is one win that I had in the past few weeks?" and "How can I celebrate this moment in my life rather than merely letting it go by?" Write down your thoughts.

Ask yourself, "What quality do I admire in others?" and "In what ways do I already have this quality, and in what ways am I building it day-to-day?" Jot down your thoughts.

Imagine your younger self looking at who you are today. What would your younger self be proud of you for?

Ask yourself, "Does my self-worth mainly come from what others think or from deep inside of me?" What would happen if you detached your worth from anything outside of yourself (e.g., other people's opinions or your work) and remembered that you are inherently worthy?

What is one thought, feeling, or bias about yourself that you want to unlearn because it's keeping you from stepping into your personal greatness (e.g., "I am not good enough to . . .")? What might help you start to unlearn this belief and begin to notice things that support a new perspective?

WEEK 18

FOCUSING ON OTHERS

Check in on someone who may be lonely today. Do one small thing to remind them that they belong and are not alone. When you've done this, reflect on the experience.

Close your eyes and spend a few minutes wishing both the people close to you and the people not so close to you well. Afterward, write down how you feel.

Choose a simple act of kindness to practice today. At the end of the day, consider how it impacted your own happiness and the happiness of the person who received it. Be mindful not to underestimate the power of a kind word or act of caring.

What is a win that someone you know has had recently? Get creative and think of a small way you can help them celebrate it today. Once you have done this, write about how you felt during and after the experience.

Ask yourself, "What is one way I can contribute to my community and do it with joy?" Take a small step to put this act of service into action today. Then reflect on how contributing to your community might contribute to your happiness.

Help someone today by lending them an ear. Listen to what's on their mind and in their heart. Make it all about offering compassion and understanding rather than opinions and solutions. How did it feel to support someone just by listening?

How do you show others you care? Write about someone you know who needs a helping hand. Find one way to be there for them and encourage them to believe in themselves today. Reflect on your experience.

WEEK 19

BUILDING SELF-CONFIDENCE

Ask yourself, "What makes me feel strong and empowered?" Reflect and write about it freely for 5 to 10 minutes.

What are some things, big or small, that you've achieved in your life? Take 10 minutes to acknowledge your past successes and brag about them. Continue on a separate sheet of paper, if you'd like.

Close your eyes for two or three minutes and imagine putting on your superhero cape. Afterward, reflect on what wearing this cape of confidence feels like on your body, what posture it comes with, and what you believe about yourself while wearing it.

What changes and improvements have you noticed in yourself over the past few weeks, few months, and year?

Write down a list of your fears. Identify and pull out two fears that you feel ready to start embracing, and write "To-Do List" above them. How can you actively begin to understand and embrace these fears rather than ignore and avoid them? Continue on a separate sheet of paper, if you'd like.

Give yourself a small challenge that you can—without a doubt—rise to today. What challenge did you choose? How did you feel after taking it on? What does it show you about who you are?

What is one thing you've been wanting to do that would require you to step out of your comfort zone a little? Where can you find the courage to do it this week? How can you surround yourself with people who will support you and build you up as you do it? (See page 166 for additional resources on finding a supportive community.)

WEEK 20

HAVING A SENSE OF PURPOSE AND MEANING

Think of something memorable that happened to you recently. What was the personal meaning of this event for you and your life? What did you learn from it?

Ask yourself, "What makes life meaningful for me?" Write your thoughts.

What gives your life a sense of purpose and motivates you? What is one way you can connect with this sense of purpose today, either at home or at work?

____

____

____

____

____

Complete this sentence: "I want to live in a world where __________." Then take a moment to remember that we create the world by creating ourselves. How can you start contributing today to the kind of world you want to live in?

____

____

____

____

____

What is something that lets you know that your life has meaning, value, and importance? Tap into how it feels as you write about it.

____

____

____

____

____

Assess your life interests by asking, "Do I like to work with people? Ideas? Things? Information?" Take 10 minutes to consciously daydream and write about the ways you can do more of what interests you in your life.

Pick one part of the day, and live it as if your only purpose in life is to do what makes you happy. What is life like when you are living it with joy as your sole mission?

WEEK 21

WELCOMING SELF-LOVE

In a healthy, loving relationship, how does one person treat the other? Commit to treating yourself in this way anytime something—good, bad, or in between—comes up this week. What was it like to treat yourself in this way?

Think about something that you're finding difficult to navigate in your life right now. What would someone who loves themselves do in this situation? What is one thing you can do to start thinking and acting like someone who loves themselves more?

Be a renegade and stop being hard on yourself. What is something you are hard on yourself for? What could you do more of if you were loving toward yourself instead?

Take a look in the mirror. As your reflection stares back at you, imagine it telling you all the things it appreciates and likes about you and why. What did your reflection say to you?

Fill in the blank: "Once I have/am ________, I will love myself." Then answer this question: "What would happen if I tried on the idea that my worth is inherent and not based on this or any other quality I think I need?"

Think of a situation that may have contributed to your thinking that you are unlovable or flawed in some way. If you could go back in time, what words would you say to yourself in that situation? Imagine yourself doing that now. How does it feel to offer yourself love in this way? (See page 166 for additional resources on self-love.)

The next time your inner critic chimes in, hear its words for what they are: hurtful phrases meant to mold you into a person who is too perfect to get hurt again. Reflect on how it affects you to acknowledge your inner critic's intentions without immediately agreeing with everything it says.

WEEK 22

TAKING RESPONSIBILITY FOR MY OWN HAPPINESS

Ask yourself, "When do I feel happiest, and why?" Knowing what you know about yourself, how can you make today the kind of day you know you will enjoy?

Fill in the blanks: "One thing I need to add to my life to experience greater happiness is ________. One thing I need to subtract from my life to experience greater happiness is ________." Explain why.

Ask yourself, "What is one thing I want to do but haven't yet done because I'm afraid to fail?" and "What do I need to know or do to feel safe in moving closer to doing this?"

If you were to start believing and acting like you were the most important person in your life, what would you do that you haven't yet done?

No matter what age you are, it's never too late to create a happier life. Imagine you are creating a new job, volunteer activity, or social activity made solely for you. What does it look like?

What is something you may not want to hear but need to hear about what's stopping you from being happier? What is one way you can encourage yourself to change this with gentleness, acceptance, and kindness?

Imagine your happiest life. What are you doing, where are you doing it, and who are you doing it with? What is one step you can take this week to get closer to this life?

WEEK 23

SEEKING PERFECTION

What are some of the reasons that drive you to seek perfection (e.g., "I don't want to fail or be rejected.")? What do you get from trying to get everything perfect?

A drive for perfection may be one of many drives you have. If another one of your drives (e.g., for purpose, connection, or hope) could—or does—provide some balance to the drive for perfection, what would it be? Write about the experience of balancing the drive for perfection with other internal drives.

How do you feel around people who have flaws? How about those who appear perfect? Reflect on what this means for you in terms of how you live your life.

What makes you imperfect? Rather than feeling defeated by this weakness or imperfection, how can you see it as an opportunity for growth or as something that makes you beautiful in ways that only you could be?

Is a desire for perfection preventing you from making progress in an area of your life? Put your hand on your heart and say, "I was made to be real, not perfect." Then choose one real, rather than perfect, action you can take today in the direction of your goals.

Let yourself off the hook today. Forget about checking everything off your to-do list, and let your day be a work in progress. How does it feel to strive more for progress and less for perfection?

Fill in the blank with a role (e.g., parent, partner, or friend) you have every day: "There is no way to be a perfect ________, but there are many ways to be a good one." At the end of the day, write about the many ways that you were good in this role without the pressure of needing to be perfect.

WEEK 24

OPENING MY HEART TO VULNERABILITY

Close your eyes and imagine your heart as consisting of various sections, some made of soft fabrics and others made of materials that have hardened over time. What is your heart made of? How much of it is soft? How much of it is hard?

You've put up some walls throughout your life, haven't you? We all have. Get curious about your walls, what caused them to go up, and what their purpose is in your life. Write about them freely.

Strong feelings, if not understood and expressed, rarely go away. What are the benefits to expressing your feelings about something that is important to you right now? What are the consequences?

Is there anything you've done in the past that you're ashamed of? How can you gather the courage today to share this with someone you love and trust, knowing that this, too, is a part of who you've been and who you are?

Write down three things about yourself you consider to be flaws. Next to each one, write down, "This, too, makes me human," as you acknowledge that every person has flaws. How does it affect you to know that it is these flaws that make you human and allow you to connect with other flawed humans?

Take 10 minutes to acknowledge one thing you need help with in your life. Who can you ask for help with this? Do you feel comfortable asking for help? If not, who or what can help you become more comfortable asking for help when you need it?

When it may not be possible to openly express how you really feel to someone, what can you do to express your feelings in an indirect way (e.g., draw or share your feelings with someone else)?

WEEK 25

LISTENING TO MY EMOTIONS

The next time you feel a noticeable emotion, replace "I am [emotion]" with "I feel [emotion]," and say it out loud. Then ask yourself, "If this emotion had a message for me, what would it be?" Write down your thoughts.

Are you feeling joyful? Great. It means you're having an experience that provides you with pleasure or meaning. Write about the meaning or pleasure that is driving this joy.

The next time you're feeling upset, ask yourself, "What is causing me hurt right now? What do I need?" Then write down one or two ways you can mindfully and intentionally tend to this hurt and its underlying need over the next few days.

Are you feeling stressed? Sit down and turn your attention inward. What message is this stress sending you about the need to slow down and practice self-care? What are one or two ways you can respond to that message over the next few days?

The next time you feel worried or anxious, ask yourself, "What doesn't feel safe right now?" Write down one or two things you can do to remind yourself that you are already safe or to create more safety in the situation.

Are you jealous of another person? Whenever you notice a feeling of jealousy this week, encourage yourself to interpret it as a sign that you want something admirable that someone else has and that you, too, have the capacity to achieve. Reflect on what this feeling means about your own desires and who you aspire to be.

Do you find yourself feeling angry? If so, pause and ask yourself, "What am I needing to defend right now—physically, emotionally, or spiritually—that is important to me?" Write about the steps you can take to defend and respect what's important to you.

WEEK 26

MANAGING AND REDUCING STRESS

How does stress show up for you? In your mind? In your body? In your actions? What do your personal and professional lives look and feel like when you're stressed?

What are some of your go-tos when it comes to managing your emotions during moments of stress? Why do these work for you?

Where is your favorite place to spend time? Does it comfort you, bring you joy, or prevent or alleviate your stress in some way? Write about it in detail as though you were sharing a photo and bragging about it to your close friends or on social media.

Is there a big task on your to-do list that feels daunting? How can you break up this big task into smaller steps? What is the first small step you can take today?

What is stressful about this week? Set a timer for five minutes and write freely about all your worries. (Use additional paper if you'd like.) When you're done, take a breath and leave your worries on the page. Reflect on how it felt to get it all out.

What is one barrier you face when trying to manage your stress effectively? Brainstorm a few ways you might try to address this barrier in the future.

____

____

____

____

____

What is one challenge you can anticipate in the coming weeks? How can you plan ahead for it this week? How does it feel to anticipate rather than avoid an upcoming challenge?

____

____

____

____

____

WEEK 27

LEARNING NEW THINGS

Who in your life serves or can serve as a mentor or role model to you? What is one thing that you are learning from this person?

What is something you can learn this week, through reading an article, listening to a podcast, or watching a video, that can help you move into the next steps of your life? Why did you choose this to learn?

How do you prefer to learn? By listening to information? Reading? Looking at visuals? Write about your brain's learning preferences. Then ask yourself, "How can I use this knowledge to help me learn what I want to learn this week?"

What is one area of your life that you feel lacks choices? Who can you talk to or what can you read or watch to expand your perspective in this area of your life?

Today, talk to someone you know with only one intention: to listen to them and learn about a viewpoint that is different from your own. Why did you choose this person, and what did you learn by listening to them?

Try a new recipe, craft, or activity today that gets you to be socially or mentally active. How does it affect your sense of joy to try to pick up a new skill or hobby?

If you saw your life as the teacher and yourself as the student, what would you say you're learning from your life right now?

WEEK 28

BOOSTING MY SENSE OF EFFICACY

What are 10 things *you* believe *you* can do?

When was the last time you succeeded at something? What was it, and what qualities and actions of yours made you capable of succeeding?

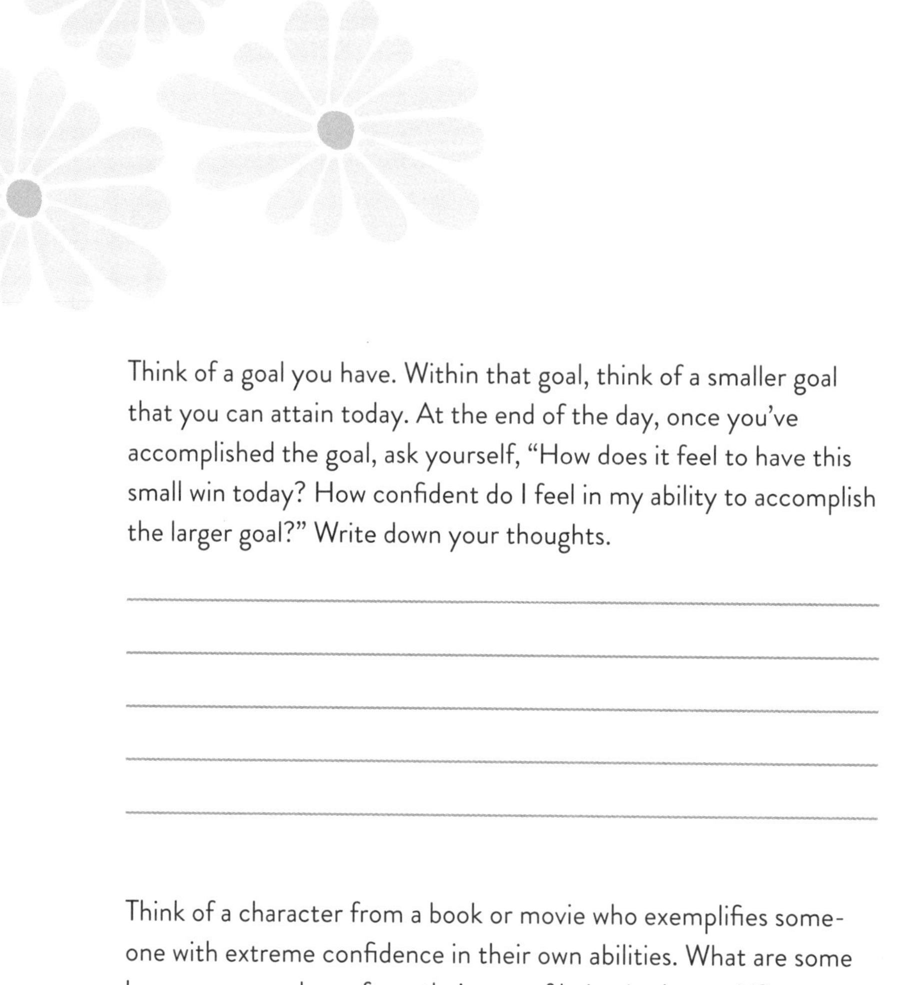

Think of a goal you have. Within that goal, think of a smaller goal that you can attain today. At the end of the day, once you've accomplished the goal, ask yourself, "How does it feel to have this small win today? How confident do I feel in my ability to accomplish the larger goal?" Write down your thoughts.

Think of a character from a book or movie who exemplifies someone with extreme confidence in their own abilities. What are some lessons you can learn from their way of being in the world?

When has investing effort and trying hard helped you solve a difficult or unforeseen problem? Reflect on and write about one such time in detail, as if you were explaining it to someone writing a book on how to solve difficult problems.

Who can you think of who is similar in many ways to you and has been successful due to their efforts in life? What does this say about your ability to be successful? (If you can't think of anyone, remember that Michael Jordan didn't make his varsity basketball team as a sophomore in high school.)

Who in your life believes in you and your ability to accomplish your goals? How can you share your goals with this person more often?

WEEK 29

MAKING TIME FOR PLAY

When was the last time you were playful? Do something creative, sporty, or musical today. Later, reflect on the difference it makes in your day when you can add a bit of play to it.

What hobbies did you have as a child or teenager? Why did you stop doing them? Tap into your younger self by engaging in one of those hobbies today. How did it feel to get back to a hobby that once brought you joy?

What is one thing you can do this week to exercise your laughing muscle? Why is it important to make time for laughter? How do you feel when you do?

If today were to be equal parts seriousness and play, what might you do differently? Is there anything you would take less seriously? Anything you would add play or humor to?

When do you feel most naturally playful? What are you doing, and who are you doing it with? How can you create more opportunities to be naturally playful in your life?

What will you do just for fun before this week ends?

Take 10 to 20 minutes today to play—doodle, dance, sing, whatever you prefer. Does play help you enjoy life more fully? Why or why not?

WEEK 30

MY SENSE OF SPIRITUALITY

Whether you consider yourself spiritual or not, is there something that brings a sense of meaning to your life beyond material or physical things? If not the word *spiritual*, what word best reflects what (or who) gives meaning to your life? (Please use this word as your personal substitute for the words *spiritual* and *spirituality* in the rest of this week's prompts.)

How do you tend to take care of your spiritual well-being? What is one way you can prioritize your spiritual well-being this week?

What do your spiritual beliefs tell you about who you are beneath all the roles you play in your life? How can you take this message with you to live your week with courage and trust?

How do you connect with your spirituality (e.g., giving thanks, praying, meditating, or spending time in nature)? How do the people in your life connect with their personal spirituality? Are any of their ways relatable to you?

If your source of spirituality were here today, what message would it have for you? How would it affect you to let the source of your spirituality guide the remainder of your day?

Can you think of a time when your spiritual well-being helped enhance your emotional well-being? What is one way your sense of spirituality can help you deal more readily with everyday challenges this week and next?

When you are connected to your sense of spirituality, how do you feel about yourself? How do you feel about others, whether strangers or friends? What effect would you say you have on the world around you?

WEEK 31

ACCOMPLISHING MY GOALS

Big goals are achieved through a series of small steps. What is one small step you can take today that will help move you in the direction of your biggest goals and dreams?

Choose one goal that you currently have. Remember your strengths (see page 16). How can you use your strengths to move closer to achieving this goal?

Ask yourself, “What is one quality I need to cultivate to grow into my fullest potential?” and “What is one step I can take now to help make it a reality?”

Choose one goal you are currently working on. Set aside worrying about doing things perfectly. What is one thing you can do *well* to make progress toward that goal this week?

Fill in the blank: “If there is one short-term desire I have that isn’t conducive to my long-term goal of happiness, it is ______.” Then write about some ways you can begin to reconcile this short-term desire with your long-term goal.

What is one area of your life that could use some improvement? What is one obstacle you can perceive to making the needed changes? Brainstorm a few possible solutions, search for help on the internet, and/or ask someone for advice.

In between all your goals is a precious thing called life. How can you enjoy your life today while also working toward your goals?

WEEK 32

PRIORITIZING SLEEP

How do you think of sleep? Is it an investment in the energy you need to successfully live tomorrow or time you'd rather spend awake? Something else altogether? Why?

Stick to a set waking time and bedtime this week. In the mornings and throughout the week, reflect on your energy level and mood. Were they the same, worse, or better than usual?

What signals does your body send you when it needs rest (e.g., low energy or trouble concentrating)? How do you typically respond? How can you bring more mindfulness to how you respond to these signals each day?

What do you need to get better sleep? A change in your environment, earplugs, or an eye mask? A mindful activity such as meditation, yoga, or a breathing exercise before bed? Something else? What support do you need in order to begin to incorporate this into your nighttime routine?

Live today with the idea that happiness is a function of getting enough sleep. Just that and nothing more. Tomorrow morning, reflect on how this idea impacted your day and your mood.

Do you notice thoughts lingering from the day? Jot them down in your journal before you go to bed. Sometimes it helps for your thoughts to have a place to go that's outside of your head.

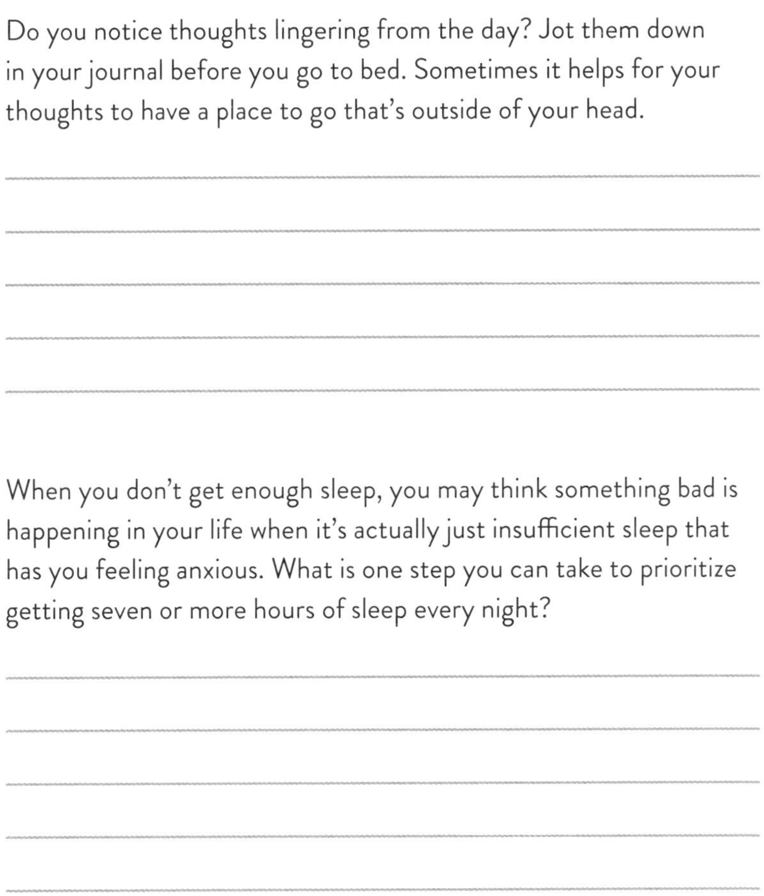

When you don't get enough sleep, you may think something bad is happening in your life when it's actually just insufficient sleep that has you feeling anxious. What is one step you can take to prioritize getting seven or more hours of sleep every night?

WEEK 33

CREATING BALANCE IN MY LIFE

Balance isn't static—it's an everyday challenge and opportunity. What would balance look like for you today?

What would life look and feel like for you if it were equal parts structure and freedom? Right now, which do you need more of and which do you need less of to create that balance?

Do you enjoy having an element of adventure in your life? If not, why not? If yes, what would it look like for your life to be simultaneously full of stability and full of adventure?

Think of a decision you need to make right now. What does your heart want you to do? What does your head want you to do? Imagine getting your head and your heart on the same page. What will your decision be?

Think of the closest relationship in your life. What are two or three ways you can balance your sense of individuality and freedom with a sense of closeness and togetherness in this relationship?

Consider the idea that sadness provides balance to happiness. When you think about your own life, what might happy moments and days give you that sad ones don't? What might sad moments and days give you that happy ones don't?

What is one behavior that is leading you to feel out of balance right now? What need was this behavior filling at the time you created it? What is a healthier way you can fill this need for yourself these days? (See page 166 for additional resources on creating balance.)

WEEK 34

GETTING INTO A STATE OF FLOW

When was the last time you were so involved in an activity that nothing else seemed to matter? What were you doing, and what helped you get into this state of flow?

Choose one activity that stretches you to engage in something challenging yet attainable today. What did you do, and how did you feel while doing it?

What is one activity you do for which your skills outweigh the challenge? How can you tweak this activity so it creates less boredom and better meets your level of skill?

To encourage a state of flow, where you're so absorbed in what you're doing that you feel fully engaged and lose track of time, find one thing you can do today to challenge yourself at the sweet spot of your skill level. What did you choose to do, and why?

Pick one task you have to do today. Rather than simply focusing on the end result, find a way to enjoy the journey. What did you do, and how did it affect you?

Today, replace one passive (low skill, low challenge) leisure activity you typically engage in (such as watching TV) with an active leisure activity that challenges you a bit more. How did doing this activity impact your state of happiness?

What is one activity you engage in, at home or at work, that is too difficult for your skill level? How can you modify this activity or do less of it so you experience less anxiety and create more potential for flow?

WEEK 35

HOW I REMEMBER MY PAST

What is one setback you've experienced in your life? Acknowledge that it hurts to experience a setback. Then visualize the full picture of your life thus far—setbacks and wins. What have setbacks meant for you in the grand scheme of your life?

What was a challenging time in your life that continues to live on within you? Let yourself be sad, glad, or mad about it for five minutes, or as long as you want. Then reflect on what made it a challenging time, what helped it to eventually work out, and what you learned about yourself during the process.

What is one mistake you made in the past that you still actively carry with you and that continues to define you today? Journal about who you would be if you no longer let your past define you in this way.

Life is full of both victories and defeats. When you look back at your life, what are two victories you've had that stand out to you?

Think back to a happy time that stood out in your life as "a moment I will remember forever." What was so special about that moment? Who was a part of it? How did you feel throughout it?

Think about a time you felt rejected by a person or group. What followed this hurtful experience of rejection? Did you eventually find a new and more suitable person to call a friend or a new group to belong to? What might the benefits be of seeing rejection as a form of redirection?

Share a past failure of yours with someone close to you and ask them if they'd be willing to do the same. Reflect on what it was like to have a shared experience that acknowledged that learning, growing, and living are inherently messy and full of failure.

WEEK 36

NOURISHING MY BODY

Rather than following rigid rules, listen to what your body wants and needs to feel nourished today. What is your stomach telling you? What is your head telling you? How do you know?

Ask yourself, "What are three things I can do this week to look after my body?" Write about it freely.

Have you made any unhelpful or unrealistic assumptions about your body (e.g., "Others won't accept me unless I look perfect," or "I'll get the same illness my mother had")? How does thinking this way affect your life? What would a more reasonable and less distressing alternative be?

Ask yourself, "If my body were my supporter and collaborator in creating a healthy, happy life, what would I do with it? How would I treat it?" Write down your thoughts.

Listen to the signals your body is sending you today. Do you feel stiffness or rigidity anywhere? What, if anything, needs tending to before it becomes something worse?

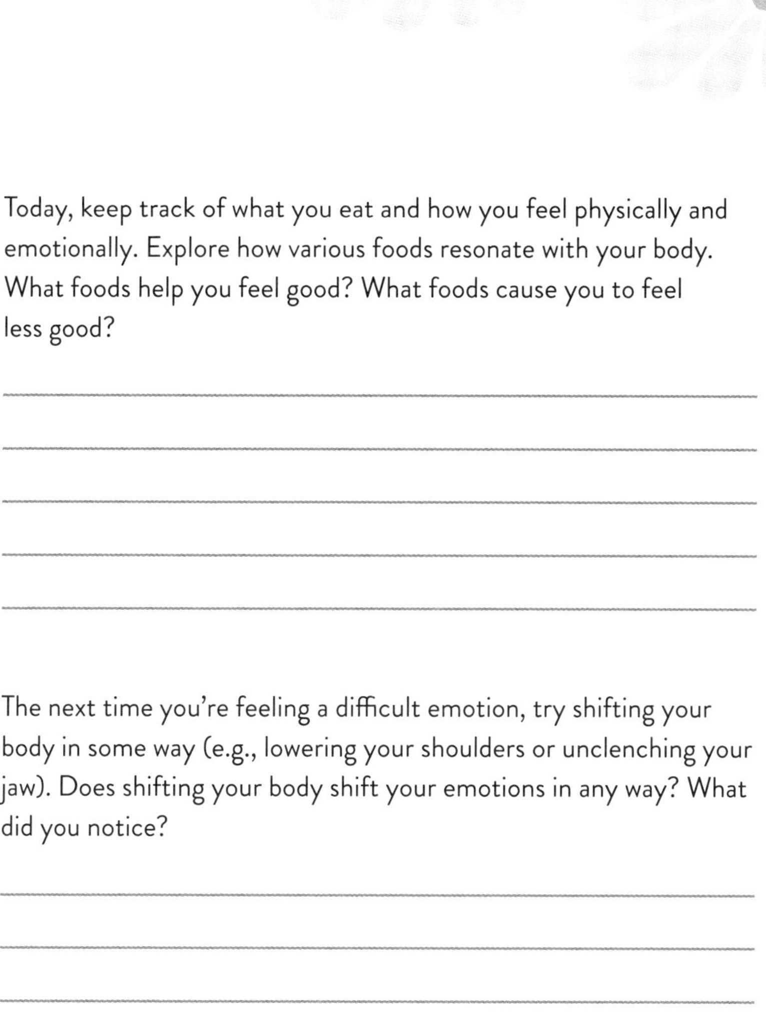

Today, keep track of what you eat and how you feel physically and emotionally. Explore how various foods resonate with your body. What foods help you feel good? What foods cause you to feel less good?

The next time you're feeling a difficult emotion, try shifting your body in some way (e.g., lowering your shoulders or unclenching your jaw). Does shifting your body shift your emotions in any way? What did you notice?

WEEK 37

CREATING A SUPPORTIVE ENVIRONMENT

Find one way to be closer to nature for 10 minutes today (e.g., go for a walk or listen to the sounds of birds). How did being closer to nature affect your mood and stress level?

Pick a space in your home and devote 15 minutes to cleaning and decluttering it. Do you think a clean space and a clear mind are related? What about a sloppy space and messy mind?

Take 10 minutes to place your favorite things where you can clearly see them in your home. After a few days, jot down the takeaways from this experience of having your favorite things in plain sight for you to enjoy.

The next time you feel stumped for a solution to a problem, go out to see some of your area's natural beauty. How does being close to nature affect your creativity and ability to solve problems?

Choose a two- or three-hour block of time to disconnect today. Turn off your phone and other devices. How did you feel immediately upon disconnecting? How did you feel a few hours later?

When you walk into your home or bedroom, do you get a joyful feeling? What can you do to inspire more joy as you walk through the door?

Is there an environment in your life that makes positive decisions feel difficult? Is there one that makes it easier and more natural to make decisions that serve you? What makes these environments so different?

WEEK 38

FEELING LOVE IN MY LIFE

Who is someone you've shared romantic or platonic love with in the past? What was special about this connection? What did it teach you about love?

Close your eyes and bring to mind a time when you felt safe and loved. What does this tell you about what's important to you when it comes to love?

Ask yourself, "What does love mean to me?" Write about it freely and with as much detail as possible.

Write about a time when you felt the love of friendship. What did it feel like, and what do you remember and cherish about this time?

Explore what your needs and desires for a romantic relationship are. Are they emotional? Physical? Social? Mental? If you need more space to reflect, continue on another sheet of paper.

Love is a noun *and* a verb. It consists of daily acts of respect and affection. How do you express love in your closest relationship (romantic or platonic)? How do you enjoy being shown love in this relationship?

Imagine that you are tasked with the responsibility of bringing more love into the world. How can you bring more love into your own life and the lives of others each day?

WEEK 39

GROWING IN SELF-AWARENESS

Think back to a recent situation with a friend, colleague, or family member that didn't go as you had hoped it would. You've likely thought about what that person could have done better or differently. What could *you* have done better or differently?

Ask yourself, "How big is the gap between what I say and what I do?" Why do you think that is? What can support you in reducing this gap?

It's time to get real with yourself. What have you been putting off or avoiding lately, and why? What is one way you can compassionately address the reasons why so you can begin to give it a try?

Imagine yourself as made of layers of emotional stress and old baggage that you've carried with you throughout your life. Beneath these layers is your true, joyous self. What one layer would it feel okay to gently start to peel to reveal more of your true self?

At the end of the day, ask yourself, "Who was I today?" Reflect and write freely and descriptively. Continue on a separate sheet of paper, if you'd like.

In what area of your life are you pointing at everyone and everything around you as the reason for why you're not living the life you want? What do you think is preventing you from taking more control in this area of your life and steering it in the direction where you want it to go?

Think back to everything that happened this week. In what situations could you have responded better? In the future, how can you support yourself in responding in a healthier way to yourself or to others?

WEEK 40

ALIGNING WITH MY VALUES

Close your eyes for a few minutes as you ask yourself, "What do I care deeply about? What do I stand for? What matters most to me in my life?" When you're done, write down 10 words or phrases that capture the essence of what you stand for and care about.

What person or situation clearly and consistently threatens your values? How would you feel, right now and in the future, if you were to gently walk away from this person or situation?

What does success mean to you? Do your goals align with your definition of success? Reflect on one thing you can do to more closely align your goals with your definition of success.

One way to know whether you're doing the "right" thing is to gauge whether your decision aligns with your values. Does your latest decision or a decision you're about to make align with your values? Why or why not?

Think about what you truly want. What do you want to do with the rest of your life? Who do you want to be? Who do you want to be around?

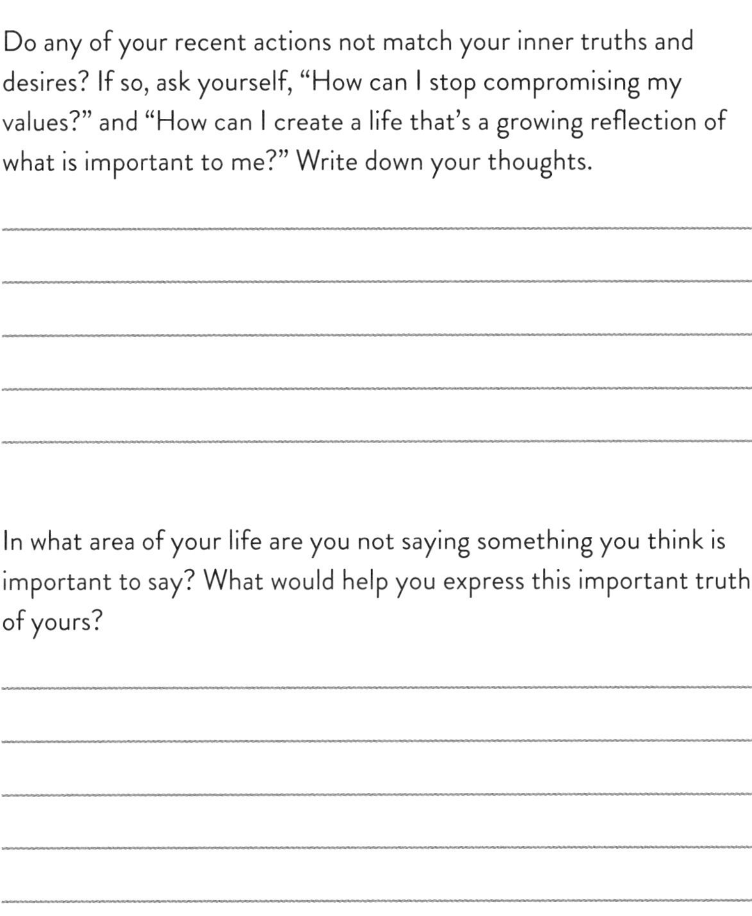

Do any of your recent actions not match your inner truths and desires? If so, ask yourself, "How can I stop compromising my values?" and "How can I create a life that's a growing reflection of what is important to me?" Write down your thoughts.

In what area of your life are you not saying something you think is important to say? What would help you express this important truth of yours?

WEEK 41

LETTING GO

To what in your life can you say, "You know, even though I prefer that it be different, this is what life is offering me right now"? How would it feel to surrender and allow life to be as it is in this way?

What are you currently trying to control that can't possibly be controlled? Take a few breaths and take a break from trying to control it. Is it possible for you to let go of your attempts to control and trust what will happen on its own? What would help you do this?

What past mistake of yours are you continuing to blame yourself for? What is one way you can stop holding yourself hostage for this mistake and start letting go of some blame?

What are you having a difficult time with this week? How can you find the courage to control what you can in the situation and simultaneously let go of what you can't change?

What old hurt have you been clinging to? If it feels safe and right for you, write a note to someone who hurt you in the past, not to share with them but to express what you think and feel. Continue on a separate sheet of paper, if you'd like. Why do you think we cling to parts of our past? Do you think there is value in giving voice to our hurts?

Who is one person you have hurt in some way? How may your actions have affected them? If you feel comfortable doing so, allow yourself to write about the emotions of guilt or remorse you feel when you bring this to mind. Remember that it is okay to feel difficult emotions sometimes.

Think back to the person you hurt in some way (from the last prompt). As you think back to what caused them pain, place your hand on your heart, remind yourself that making mistakes and feeling guilt is something everyone experiences, and offer yourself compassion for what happened. How does it feel to offer yourself compassion for this mistake? (See page 166 for additional self-compassion resources.)

WEEK 42

PRACTICING MINDFULNESS

For two minutes, focus on your breathing. As your mind wanders and thoughts come up, notice them without judgment and gently return your attention to your breath. How does it feel to intentionally choose where your attention goes?

Move from doing to being by asking yourself, "Where am I right now?" "How am I right now?" and "What am I thinking right now?" After, write about any differences you notice in your mind, body, and emotions.

Imagine your mind as a vast sky and your thoughts as clouds passing through it. How do you typically think of your thoughts? What is it like to think of your thoughts as clouds passing through a vast sky?

Choose a mantra (word or phrase) that resonates with you (e.g., peace, love, or om). Set a timer for five minutes and direct your focus to your chosen mantra. Every time your mind wanders off, gently acknowledge it and return to your mantra. When the time is up, reflect on how it felt to pause and take time to be mindful today.

Light a candle in a quiet, dimly lit room. Sit comfortably a few feet away from the candle, rest your attention at about eye level on the flame, and focus on the light for five minutes. Do you notice any differences after doing this short mindfulness meditation?

Set a timer for five minutes. Close your eyes and scan your body by bringing your attention to each part of it, one by one, from your head to your toes. Without judgment, notice any sensation that may be there, whether pleasant or unpleasant. After, reflect on the experience of being aware of and present with your body.

Choose one of the mindfulness practices from the past week to practice again. What about this practice appeals to you? How do you think practicing it might affect your ability to be more present and less distracted in your life? (See page 166 for additional meditation resources.)

WEEK 43

HOW I START MY DAY

How do you want to feel this week? What would help you welcome this new week in the way you hope to feel throughout it?

The first 20 minutes of your day set the stage for the rest of it. Do you need to add anything to, or subtract something from, your morning routine to support yourself in embracing the day with joy, courage, and ease?

What are five things you can appreciate about the start of a new day?

What is your intention for today? What kind of day do you want to have? What will you bring into this day, and what do you hope this day will bring to you?

____

____

____

____

____

Before you do something for your children, partner, colleagues, or boss today, what is one thing you can do for yourself?

____

____

____

____

____

As you get out of bed, ask yourself, "What troubles and worries of yesterday can I leave behind to start today as though it is truly the new day that it is?" Record your thoughts.

Ask yourself, "What in my life enlivens me so much that I am eager to jump out of bed in the morning?" If nothing comes to mind, try repeating the exercises from weeks 20 and 22.

WEEK 44

EMBRACING CHANGE

Think back to an unexpected change you experienced in the past five years. How did it feel to go through it? How did it feel a few months and years later? What meaning does this change have in the larger picture of your life today? Continue on another sheet of paper, if you'd like.

Sometimes if we avoid change, we also avoid personal growth and happiness. Be honest with yourself: What is one way in which you are currently avoiding change?

What or who have you outgrown in recent months or years, and why? Have you taken or do you need to take any sort of action to honor this change and growth? If so, what?

You don't need to *leap* forward into the next phase of your life—you can simply take one small step. In what area of your life do you think moving forward and making a change may be helpful, even if the change might be uncomfortable or very small at first?

To get different results, you've got to make different choices. Where in your life do you want different results? What one different choice do you think can help you get there?

Sometimes it helps us to get honest about what may no longer be working in our lives that once was. What one door can you begin to close today because it isn't leading you quite where you thought it would?

Choose a role you've taken on in recent years (e.g., parent, partner, caregiver, or student). How has taking on this role positively changed your relationship with yourself and your life?

WEEK 45

EMBRACING THE EXPERIENCES THAT SHAPED ME

Ask yourself, "Who or what made me?" Reflect and write freely for 5 to 10 minutes. Continue on a separate sheet of paper, if you'd like.

Think about all the people you've loved throughout your life. Whether they stayed for a short while or are still in your life, how has each of them shaped who you are today?

Ask yourself, "How have my culture and ethnicity shaped my identity? How have they shaped how I see myself, others, and the world? How can I honor and celebrate these aspects of myself today?" Write down your thoughts.

Think about all the places you've been in your life. How has each one shaped who you are today?

Look back at your life. What is one hard time that contributed to who you are today? What strength and/or wisdom did you gain from it? What would it be like to both hold compassion for the experience and celebrate who you are for having made it through it?

What physical or emotional scar have you developed over the course of your life? If it were to carry a message of persevering and overcoming for you, what would it be? What is one area of your life where this message can offer you hope and encouragement right now?

What is one experience from your past you considered insignificant for a long time? How has this experience shaped your future in a noticeable way, positively or negatively? How can you honor it as an important part of your personal history today?

WEEK 46

BRIDGING THE GAP BETWEEN WHO I AM AND WHO I WANT TO BE

Plan something this week for an upcoming weekend or next month (e.g., a massage or dinner with a friend). How does having something to look forward to affect how you feel?

Fill in the blank: "One way I can transform my future by what I think and do today is ________." At the end of the day, reflect on the experience of actively playing a role in shaping your future through the choices you made today.

What is one thing you can appreciate today about *where you are* in your life's journey? What is one thing you can appreciate today about *where you're heading*? If the answers don't come easily, try to dig a little deeper.

There is joy in the destination of happiness. There is also joy to be found as you grow and evolve during the journey. How would you describe the joy in the destination? How would you describe the joy that can be found along the way—and how can you find that joy today?

If today were the end of something and the beginning of something else, what would it be the end and beginning of? Record your thoughts with as much detail as possible.

You can be proud of yourself when you achieve a goal. You can also take time to be proud of yourself every step along the way, including today. Pause and tell yourself, "I am so proud of you and how far you've come." Then write freely about what pausing to be proud means to you.

What you've experienced in your life through today is what your story has been so far. But there is much more to be written. How do you intend to fill up the rest of the pages of the story of your life?

WEEK 47

MAKING IT ALL OKAY

It's okay to start over if you want or need to. If something didn't go well yesterday (or this week, month, or year), let yourself start over and try something different today. What are you starting over with, and how?

The next time you want to cry, let yourself cry. Sadness wants to be felt, sometimes through tears. How did it feel to express your sadness through tears without holding back?

Have you ever resigned yourself to not being happy? Ask yourself why, and whisper to yourself, "Hey, it's okay to be happy." What is your response to being given permission to be happy?

Reach out to someone you know and trust today. Share your personal, professional, or spiritual challenges and ask them for support. What do you need support with right now, and how can courageously asking for support from the right person help you?

It's okay to be different. Pick one thing that makes you uniquely you and act on it this week. How does it affect you to know it's okay to allow yourself to be your uniquely beautiful and original self?

The next time you're not feeling okay, take the time you need to think, feel, rest, process, and be human. It's okay to not feel okay. Reflect on how it feels to know that not being okay from time to time is part of being human.

The next time you're going through a tough time, be gentle with yourself. Write a note letting yourself know that you will get through this tough time like you've gotten through others before. Remind yourself that whatever you're going through is part of life and won't last forever.

WEEK 48

HOW I WANT TO BE REMEMBERED

Imagine someone is writing a book about your life. What are a few of the memories and people you would like included in this book?

What are three things about yourself you wish others knew? How can you share these things with people more often and readily?

Describe two people who have changed your life. What qualities of theirs do you hope to carry with you?

If you could be remembered for either your level of kindness or your level of success, which would you choose, and why?

If you were to live today in the way you want to be remembered, what is one thing you would do, and why?

How do you hope the young people in your life (e.g., your own children, nieces, nephews, students, or neighbors' children) will remember their childhood?

When you look back, what impact (at home, through your work, or in your community) do you want to have made on the world?

WEEK 49

SAVORING LIFE'S EXPERIENCES

For about five minutes, think about a pleasant memory that has personal meaning to you. Focus your attention on the pleasure the experience brought you—the people involved and the things you saw, heard, and felt. Write about how it felt to replay this memory.

Think of something good that happened recently. Talk or text about it with someone you haven't shared it with. Tell them what made it feel good. Then reflect on how it felt for you to share this experience with someone.

Take 5 to 10 minutes to reminisce about a positive experience. When you're done, give this experience some room in your daily life by displaying a photo or an object that reminds you of it. What impact does reminiscing in this way have on your sense of happiness?

Take an extra 5 to 10 minutes in bed. As you're lying there, think about how lucky you are to be enjoying these wonderful moments. What stood out to you the most from this extra time in bed?

In your head, replay the moments of the last joyful experience you had in the company of family, friends, or a romantic partner. Write about the most memorable part.

Cook or order one of your favorite meals. Eliminate all distractions and let your senses get fully absorbed in eating this meal. Reflect on what it was like to savor a meal in this way.

Today, take a photo of an experience you're having. Let taking the photo help you notice a different aspect of the experience instead of disconnecting you from it. Describe what you noticed.

WEEK 50

INTEGRATING MY PAST WITH MY PRESENT

Imagine your life as a movie. What scenes have been your favorite? What scenes do you wish you could delete?

In the movie of your life, you can't actually go back and delete scenes. However, you can make sense of and honor them. Pick one scene you wish you could delete, and instead of grabbing scissors, write about everything you felt and wish you could have said or done that you didn't say or do then.

What words do you wish someone would say to you when you're going through a tough time? Think back to a tough time when there was no one to say those words to you. Imagine saying those words to yourself. What is it like to offer something to yourself *now* that you wish you had heard and felt *then*?

Think of a situation in the past when you felt unheard or misunderstood. How did it make you feel? What truth did you wish could be heard but wasn't? How can you offer yourself now the understanding that you'd hoped for then?

Think about something you regret. If that happened today, what would you do differently? Whenever it feels true and unforced, write yourself a message of compassion for doing the best you could with what you knew and were able to do then.

Break the (internal) silence. Write about something important to you that you've never spoken about before. What happened, how did it affect you, and what do you want to remember from this event in your life?

What is your first memory of disliking some part of yourself? What happened, and how did it feel? How can you help yourself reinterpret what happened and offer yourself compassion for having had that hurtful experience?

WEEK 51

HONORING MYSELF

What one thing in your life isn't working for you anymore? What single step can you take to change or stop it? This is how you honor yourself, bit by bit.

Is there a need you've been waiting for someone else to fill for you (e.g., a need to feel loved, safe, or validated)? What is it, and what is one way you can begin to meet this need yourself today?

Everyone connects with their intuition differently (e.g., by journaling or practicing mindfulness). What is one way you can connect with your intuition today? What do you think it is telling you, and how can you honor what it is telling you today?

What upcoming situation do you feel worried or unsettled about? How can you anticipate your needs in this situation and honor them right now as you look ahead?

Think of a person in your life whose behavior you're not okay with. What values or needs of yours does the behavior rub up against? Is there a need you have to express or a boundary you want to set? What would it be like to communicate this boundary to this person?

Have you ever felt mistreated but not said anything? How has not voicing your needs or setting a boundary affected you? What would it be like to stand up for yourself, knowing it may be uncomfortable at first but important to you?

Honoring yourself through self-care is an ongoing learning process that never ends. Ask yourself, "What is one way I can give myself permission to make time to practice self-care today?"

WEEK 52

PUTTING IT ALL TOGETHER

Reflecting on your journey throughout this journal, how would you define happiness? What does happiness mean to you?

Reflecting on the activities you've done and reflections you've had throughout the course of using this journal, what do you know about what makes you happy? What makes sense for you to do more of in the future?

Reflecting on the time you've spent with this journal, what do you know about what makes you less happy? What do you intend to do less of in the future because it reduces your happiness?

What is one activity you've explored in this journal that can help you ride the waves life will undoubtedly bring and that you can put in your happiness toolbox?

What is one piece of knowledge you've gained throughout this journal that has helped you get through a hard time and that you can use to bring a little more happiness to yourself as time goes on?

What have you learned through your journaling about how you can approach the things that might seem to be wrong with you or different about you? What discoveries about yourself will you take with you as you move forward?

What is one message that captures the light-bulb moments you've had while using this journal? Write it in BIG letters. Why is it important to carry this message forward and offer it to yourself today, tomorrow, and every day?

CLOSING THOUGHTS

You came, you sought, and you tried on new ideas. You did new things, dove deep into your inner world, examined your outer world, and gained new ways of being, doing, and living life that help you cultivate happiness. Hopefully through it all you've learned that happiness isn't something you either do or don't have. Rather, it's a verb consisting of choices and actions, a feeling you can return to any time, and most important, a way of being and believing that is and always has been inside of you.

So what's next?

Your journey doesn't end here. As you keep living these 52 aspects of happiness, you will undoubtedly discover more about who you are and what you need in order to be genuinely happy. You will become even more confident. You'll let go of the judgment that you shouldn't feel the way you do. You will learn to love yourself in ways you didn't think were possible. You will integrate parts of yourself that have long been stuck in the past. You will begin to love others more deeply. You'll create space to do more of the things that make you happy and toss away those that don't. You'll create more support around you. You'll achieve your heart's desires, make mistakes, learn new things, relearn others, and grow deeper in genuine happiness from it all.

I invite you to come back to this journal and use it as your guide throughout the course of your life. The questions we ask ourselves as we journey to greater and deeper happiness remain the same, though our personal answers may change. That's the beautiful thing about it—the journey never ends. As you grow and nurture your happiness, it only gets better.

Know that what you do makes a 100 percent difference. One person's joy affects a family's joy. A family's joy affects a community's joy. A community's joy amplifies the joy of a country, and a country's joy amplifies the joy of the world. From my heart to yours, thank you for being you and for embracing the vulnerable, courageous, fun, and sometimes messy moments along the road to happiness.

"Happiness turned to me and said—
'It is time. It is time to forgive yourself for
all of the things you did not become. It is
time to exonerate yourself for all of
the people you couldn't save, for all of
the fragile hearts you fumbled with in the
dark of your confusion. It is time, child,
to accept that you do not have to be who
you were a year ago, that you do not have
to want the same things. Above all else,
it is time to believe with reckless
abandon that you are worthy of me,
for I have been waiting for years.'"

—BIANCA SPARACINO, *SEEDS PLANTED IN CONCRETE*

References

Dowrick, Stephanie. *Choosing Happiness: Life and Soul Essentials*. Australia: Allen & Unwin Academic, 2005.

Sparacino, Bianca. *Seeds Planted in Concrete*. Brooklyn, New York: Thought Catalog Books, 2015.

Resources

The following resources have been created to support you as you incorporate insights from this journal into your life:

The Guide to Happier (and Stronger) Relationships

The Daily Guide to Self-Love

Mindfulness Meditation

Self-Compassion Meditation

A Simple Guide to Creating Balance in Your Life

To access the resources, please visit TheHappinessDoctor.com/guides.

To help you get the most out of your journal experience, you are also invited to join our supportive community working with the 52 topics presented in this book. To join the community, please visit TheHappinessDoctor.com/community.

Acknowledgments

To all the people who make my world a happy one just by being in it—

Mila, Lenya, Sonia, and Felix: I admire, cherish, and love you deeply. My parents, Izabella and Anatoly: Your understanding and support constantly permeate my heart. My dear friends Kristen, Tieg, Kristen, and Laura: Your bountiful love and encouragement weave a constant string of joy throughout my life. My partner, Joe: Your patience, softness, and understanding give me so much to be grateful for. I love you. Shiloh: Thank you for being an anchor of the sweetest joy there is. You forever have a special place in my heart. Big Bro: I am so honored to share a deep trust with you. My life is so special because you're in it. To all my dear friends, colleagues, clients, and everyone who cares, shares, and whose heart connects with mine in small or big ways who wasn't individually named here: I deeply thank you.

And to every single one of you: My heart is so full knowing that you picked up this book and made its wisdom a part of your life. Today, I pass on to you seven words that I wrote to myself a number of years ago:

I love you.

And you got this.

About the Author

Sophia Godkin, PhD, is a health psychologist, happiness and relationship coach, bestselling author, and internationally recognized expert on happiness. Better known as "The Happiness Doctor," Dr. Sophia helps people develop unwavering confidence, create satisfying relationships, and become genuinely happy no matter their past and no matter their current circumstances. Whether in the form of individual and group coaching, writing, or courses, Dr. Sophia is known for the depth, lightheartedness, and transformative potential of her work. She is also the author of *The 5-Minute Gratitude Journal*. Visit her online and join her ever-growing community of people on their path to greater happiness at TheHappiness-Doctor.com.